Dub's Dandy Inventions

Dub's Dandy Inventions

A look into the preciousness of a little boy

Eric Ludy

Bravehearted PRESS
WINDSOR, COLORADO

Dub's Dandy Inventions:
A look into the preciousness of a little boy

by Eric Ludy

Copyright © 2017 by Eric Ludy

All Scripture quotations are from: The Holy Bible, King James Version. Public Domain.

ISBN 978-1-943592-50-0 (paperback)

Bravehearted Press
655 Southwood Lane | Windsor, CO 80550

Published in the United States of America.
First Edition, 2015
Second Edition, 2017

BraveheartedChristian.com

Dedication

For Dub, of course.

CONTENTS

INTRODUCING DUB

This is Dub

My little six-year-old was given the very formidable and regal-sounding first name of Kipling. My dad's philosophy on boy names was simply, "If you can't imagine it as the name of a U.S. President, then don't stick it like a banner to the forehead of your son!" My father wanted his sons to grow up with a sense of dignity and purpose.

Naming me "Eric Winston" was his way of sticking me in a power tie when I was one day old.

Subconsciously, I think I adopted my dad's thinking on the matter. I want to name my boys something epic and strong – something that they can catch a vision for and grow up to become. The name "Kipling" just fit the bill for this little guy. It has the hint of poet with the strong cologne of a boxing champion woven into the fabric of its cadence. And, yes, "Vote Kipling come November" just works. A nation wants a man at the helm that has the sensitivity of a literary master and yet carries a big Rooseveltian stick in his pocket.

When Kipling was christened "Kipling Joel Anthony Ludy" on November 1st, 2008, my father instinct for the epic and the strong was satisfied. I leaned back in my easy chair and toasted the air with my imaginary glass of sparkling cranberry juice, declaring, as if prophetically, "You will be a man, my son!"

Kipling arrived home from the hospital on Election Day 2008, the very same day a man named "Barack" was elected to office. Who would have ever guessed that a guy with the name "Barack" would ever become a U.S. President? I guarantee you: my dad would have never guessed it. And, it so happens that this very day, November 4th, 2008, was also the day that Kipling's epic and strong name simply disappeared. I had hardly time to set down my glass of sparkling cranberry juice before his name was no more. It was as if once a "Barack" could be elected president, pandemonium broke out in the name-world underground. Any boy's name was now a possibility for stardom. Eugene, Duane, Dilbert, and Egbert were all suddenly just as probably the next name of a president as William, George, John, or Thomas.

And, maybe this is why I allowed it. I'm not sure. I still question my paternal judgment on the matter. But, something about the weird and shocking disorder to that Super-Tuesday caused me to concede – it caused me to let go of the manly Ludy naming heritage.

We arrived home from the hospital carrying that little bundle of cuteness. Kipling was wearing his power tie, and Daddy was cooing his epic and strong name into his ear, confident that the more he heard its majestic and poetic cadence the quicker he would form into a man worthy of such a valiant moniker. But, in the midst of this serene and precious scene, a little almost-two-year old named Harper Grace Ludy spoke. And her words…well…they destroyed the manly name of "Kipling" forever.

"My Baby Dubber!" she said, attempting to peek inside the car seat carrier. Her voice was so sweet. Her eyes laughing with delight.

She was trying to say, "My Baby Brother," but her speech impediments at the age of twenty-one months caused her to unwittingly re-christen our little four-day-old man-in-the-making.

"Baby Dubber" stuck. It was so cute. It was a chubby, strawberry-jam-on-the-cheek sort of name that fit this little wonder boy. So, I, the protector of the manly heritage and potential of my little boy, allowed it to be utilized as the name of choice inside the Ludy household. At the time I didn't realize that in doing so it would thoroughly replace the other name – you know the one that I had so carefully and prayerfully chosen.

Baby Dubber was a name of great potential with a surprising amount of elasticity and moldability. Quickly it began to morph. Double-Blubber-Dubber was an early entry into the contest. Dubber-doo, Dubber-dooster, Dubber-dooey, Dubster, Dubby, Dubbies, Doost, The Doost, The Doosty-Dandy, and Dubs all were worthy entries into the renaming of my son. And, I must admit, all of the just-mentioned have each been used many times over the past six years. But just plain "Dub" is the one that has stuck out above all the others. Much to my chagrin, it's the little dude's name now. "Who is Kipling?" most people say. "The only one here is Dub!"

So, we can thank Barack for pioneering the way for names like Eugene, Duane, Dilbert, Egbert, and even Dub to one day make their way into U.S. history books as bonafide future Presidents of the United States. Sure, Obama may have brought us some things we didn't really want, but just think – he also brought me as a father the ability to see that odd names can have really big futures.

DUB, THE LITTLE RASCAL

Dub is a memorable sort of little boy. I wish I could take credit for it, but since he was adopted, I always feel a bit awkward when I start claiming genetic influence over his life.

He's sort of like a black-and-white Little Rascals character. He's always busy. Busy of mind and busy of body. In his second year of life I recognized that I was in need of a deeper sanctification, for frustration and irritation were constant companions in my soul when dealing with this little guy. If I said, "Stay in bed, Dub!" he would somehow hear, "Quickly, Dub, get out of bed, crawl under the bed, carve into the bed frame, get wedged in, and then scream at the top of your lungs for Daddy to come back in two minutes later to help get you unstuck."

But, with all of his rascally quirks, he is truly something special. He is possibly the most affectionate and expressive of our six children. He is well-known throughout the Ludy house for his spontaneous declarations of genuine encouragement.

"I love you, Mommy!"

"Daddy, you are a great Daddy!"

"Hudson, your Lego model is amazing!"

"You are so pretty, Harper!"

"Avy, you look just like a Princess!"

"Do you know that Lily has the cutest belly-button ever!"

"Rees sure is being obedient today, Daddy! Good job, Rees!"

This little guy seems to be the perfect mix of poet and boxer. I never would have guessed that the name Dub could offer him the same potential as the name Kipling, but it seems it has. There is just more boxer in the name "Dub" than I originally was bargaining for. If we could change his name to Dublin, that would probably balance it out, but it just wouldn't be him anymore. He really is "Dub."

DUB, THE INVENTOR

Did I mention that Dub is an avid inventor? Oh, he's not quite the refined DaVinci yet; he's more Dub-inchy. NOTE: Sorry about the terrible Dub-inchy pun (that was put in there for my dear friend Dan, who would have said it if I didn't write it).

Dub doesn't yet have a clue how to actually build any of his grand ideas, but he does know how to express them at the breakfast table after lying in his bed all night thinking about them.

Some might consider Dub's ideas a little like Emmit's Double-Decker Couch, and I would say they are probably right. You just get the idea that what you are hearing is so utterly ridiculous that God might smile and make one of them really happen.

I was an inventor when I was young, too. And though I can't take genetic credit for Dub's inventiveness, I do feel a kinship with his anything-is-possible-for-those-who-simply-believe attitude.

When Dub first turned five years old, he went on a seven-week invention binge. I missed a few of these grand ideas, but after a few days I began writing them down.

This book is sort of a memorial to the little guy. Herein are the twelve brilliant Dandy Dub Inventions that spurted out of his little noggin in the seven weeks following his fifth birthday.

If you asked me why I wrote this, I might say, "Because I didn't want to forget it." But, there is more to it than that. I wrote this as a testimony of my tender and affectionate fatherly love for a little boy that God providentially stuck into my life and gave me the grace to call my very own son. There are a lot of folks out there that are considering adopting, but they are afraid their affections for an adopted child wouldn't or couldn't be as strong as towards a biological child. That's pure hogwash. Just read this and you will say to yourself, "I want to have a Dub in my life, too!" And I would agree with you. What's there not to love?

Give me forty Dubber-Doosters!

Gulp! Did I just write that?

INVENTION ONE

The Robot Trickster

Bedtime in the Ludy home is big deal. Each child has sort of developed their own personalized traditions with Mommy and Daddy. Some of our children want a song, some just want to snuggle in the rocking chair, and some want a book read to them. Dub usually wants to talk (albeit with Daddy he always wants to finish the conversation with a tickle session). Dub is a talker. This little guy has around fifty thousand words a day he needs to get out, and bedtime is usually when he cranks out about thirty thousand of them. If Mommy and Daddy are prepared, this "bed time routine" is a great time to chronicle Dub inventions.

Leslie and I have noticed that children really do say the darndest things. The problem is, out of every five great quotables, we usually only write down around one of them. Oh, for the day when Dub invents a machine that captures every cute Ludy kid quotable and memorializes it for all posterity.

For every invention detailed in this book, there have easily been an additional four that have gone unwritten. But, instead of crying over spilled milk, let's cherish the milk that's still in the cup. And let's start this off with the famed "Robot Trickster." Though this is certainly not Dub's first invention, history may in fact show that it was. For it was the first one that Leslie and I wrote down.

It was a cozy, snuggly evening in early December of 2013. Momma was tucking the little dude in and Dub was on fire with ideas. As Momma talked with him, he was squirming like a wild man under the covers. He had just figured out the concept of "playing tricks" on his brothers and sisters. Playing tricks on siblings is definitely not a concept that we prosper and propagate as parents, but it's amazing how kid's pick up these rascally concepts in their growing up years, no matter how hard we try and keep them ignorant of foolish behavior.

Dub had a juicy and exciting plan doing backflips inside his little mind. It was a plan he intended to execute once Mommy left the room, the lights were turned off, and all was clear. He knew he probably shouldn't tell Momma of his nighttime, after-hours plans, but Dub suffers from a funny disability – he can't keep the thoughts twirling inside his mind from shooting off his tongue. And so, to his dismay, out the juicy and exciting plan came. Dub divulged his sneaky plan to tip-toe down the hall into Hudson and Harper's rooms while they were sleeping and play tricks on them.

Even as he said it out loud, Dub was hitting

himself for allowing the idea to go airborne. But airborne it went. Momma, stifling a smirk as only the best mommas can do, gently informed him, in no uncertain terms, that there would be no sneaking, and no playing tricks on his two older siblings.

Dub, quite disappointed in the news from Momma, instantly went to work, crafting another idea. After all, as the old adage goes, "Necessity is the mother of invention." And, certainly, Dub was in a situation of great necessity.

This precise situation was the seed bed of Dub's first recorded invention.

"Momma," Dub said with a twinkle in his eye. "I'm going to make a robot that can sneak out of bed and play tricks for me."

Brilliant. What an amazing market there is for the "other you" that can do all your sinning for you.

I must admit, it wasn't Dub that invented the idea of the "Alter Ego," but he sure did put a new face on it with his Robot Trickster invention.

If you, like Dub, have that sneaky side to you, then maybe you should order a print of Dub's "Robot Trickster," frame it, hang it on the wall where you can see it every day, with "the parent-edition" of 1 Corinthians 13:6 written underneath it:

Love does not delight in sneaking out of bed and playing tricks on others but rejoices in staying in bed and getting a good night's sleep.

1 Corinthians 13:6
(or, at least, the gist of it)

INVENTION TWO

The Ride of Your Life

Dub's second recorded invention occurred a week later at the breakfast table.

Dub and breakfast have a unique relationship. He almost always calls breakfast "dinner" – so, it seems breakfast gets back at him by sticking a little something extra into his eggs. The word "hyper" might be fitting for Dub in the morning.

It's a tradition for Daddy to start out breakfast by asking Dub to sit down, settle down, be still, and be quiet. But since the little guy has so much to share that the idea of being "quiet" is hard for him to grasp. So, Daddy, only moments after the prayer is finished, usually has to institute the "quiet rule" over the breakfast table. It works like this. I declare, "If anyone has something they would like to share, then they must raise their hand. There will be no talking until you are called upon." NOTE: *It's a great rule.* At the inauguration of the "quiet rule," Dub will shoot up his hand high into the air.

Daddy will usually pause for a few seconds in order to look about the table in hopes that someone a bit more calm could be called upon. Sometimes Lily will chime in with some news about Rees's bib not being put on properly, her fork having dropped on the floor, or the fact that she loves eggs. But this sort of fluff material can only fill time for so long. Before long, it is time to unleash Dub.

"Yes, Dub?" I respond, in a slow, serene voice, purposely adding a professional dignity to the atmosphere in hopes that it will set a more calm tone and dignified model for him to pattern his speaking style after when he does start talking. I'm not sure that my calming strategy has actually ever proven to have any real effect upon this little fireball.

"Daddy, Daddy, Daddy!" he yells. He has so much bottled-up that one "Daddy" is not enough. It's like a traffic jam of words that has been created while waiting for Daddy to let him move forward. It's rush hour in Dub Ludyville, and Daddy has closed down all four lanes of traffic on the main interstate through the city with this crazy "quiet rule."

Such was the scene in mid-December of 2013. Dub had just yelled out, "Daddy, Daddy, Daddy!" and the Niagaran flow of words was about to commence. Papa Ludy had once again created a traffic jam on I-5 through Dub Ludyville by my attempts at calming the little guy down.

"Daddy, Daddy, Daddy!" he blurted out again, as I officially called on his raised hand. "I have an idea! Do you want to hear it? It's a really good idea! It's about a ride! Do you want to hear it?"

When attempting to properly punctuate a Dub-spoken sentence I struggle to be accurate and true to history. I'm not one that likes to use more than one exclamation mark at the conclusion of an individual sentence. I guess you could say that it feels somewhat juvenile to pile on a whole series of exclamation marks, when one exclamation mark would do just fine. In fact, in six consecutive sentences, it is against my better judgment to use more than one exclamation mark in total over that stretch of text for concern of emotional over-exaggeration. However, in the six Dub-spoken sentences in the previous paragraph, I believe five exclamation marks would be perfectly at home at the conclusion of each of the sentences spoken and I would be judged right and just in the courts of literary license and grammatical propriety.

With Dub desperately attempting to unclog the traffic on I-5, I told him that I would love to hear his idea.

At this removal of roadblocks and orange traffic cones, Dub put his foot on the gas and began to scream down the interstate.

Here is my best attempt at capturing his words verbatim. Words spoken, mind you, without a breath.

Since Dub speaks like a machine gun, it makes sense that I would put his subsequent statements into bullet points (again, Dan, that pun was for you):

- *I'm going to make a ride called Fire Exploding!*
- *It's a really fast ride that goes down like "this"* (his little five-year-old hand swooped down and his face made a grimace as if it

was experiencing, as he spoke, the terrifying drop in altitude being currently described)

- *And it goes down into the fire, where there are knights standing in the fire that move like "that"* (he shows me the dangerous and fearful movement of the knights as they draw their swords and threateningly point them at the shocked riders of the ride – his cute little face bursting forth with animation as if it were on fire, reminding me that fire is everywhere at this stage of the ride)
- *And there is a huge mountain with a mountain lion on it that blows* (at this he blows like a mountain lion – which by the way, for those of you who have never witnessed a mountain lion blowing – is a very powerful form of blowing)
- *And it blows your sled* (this is when I realized that this is a sled-based ride, kind of like such famous rides as the Matterhorn, It's a Small World, or Splash Mountain)
- *And this leads you into a cave, where there are knights with pokey helmets on* (not to be confused with the knights standing in the fire, mentioned previously)
- *And there will be dinosaurs and dinosaur fossils in there, too* (Why not? Knights and dinosaur fossils are perfectly compatible)
- *It's a scary ride that gives you a headache, and that's why it is only for big persons. It also makes you really dizzy.*

Such a ride fits Dub. Here he is, just newly five years old, and he is inventing a ride for Momma and Daddy to ride. He's just fine waiting at the exit for the two of us to come stumbling out, stomach in hand, to hear how fun it all was. He won't be able to ride it probably until he's 48 inches tall, and yet, he's lying in bed all night long dreaming of a gift he can give to all his favorite "big persons."

Even though it sounds like I may get a headache and a bit dizzy through the grand theatrical adventure, I'm game.

I want to clarify, Dub is not all sneaking and tricking. He's also a big pile of gift-giving affection.

Thank you, Dub, for Fire Exploding. I will always treasure this gift of near-death terror that you dreamed up for me.

INVENTION THREE

The Big Bead Maker

Back in mid-December of 2013, our four year old girl, Avy (short for Avonlea), was officially outlawed from playing with little beads. Leslie had purchased a whole box full of little beads for the kids with which to make special crafts and Avy loved these little things. And, now, after having picked the entire box of them up off the wood floor in the kitchen, the carpet in the classroom, her bed, and the floor of our home office, all at different times, it had become apparent to me that little Avy was not yet old enough to know how to properly handle these little beads.

I declared her official banishment from beads sometime when I had arrived home that night from work and subsequently found the entire collection of little things all over the kitchen wood floor.

"Avy!" I declared with fatherly finality. "You are no longer allowed to play with these little beads. I have asked you to handle them with greater care and watchfulness, but you have time and again let them dump all over the place. And Daddy is the one always left picking them up."

In the shadows, a little boy named Dub lurked, listening in to this chastening. He was deeply moved with compassion for his little four-year-old sister and could hardly imagine how hard this would be on her. He knew that Avy loved those little beads. He pondered in his mind what it would be like to lose the privilege of playing with Legos (his little bead equivalent), and he could hardly stand it.

So, in the shadows the little hero went to work on an invention.

At the dinner table that night, Dub bravely voiced that he had overheard the Avy banishment from all forms of playing with little beads. The pain in his voice was obvious. This little guy was aching, longing for something to be given to Avy that would fill in that gigantic void that Daddy's heartless denials had created.

This is when the Ludy family heard Dub's third invention.

"I'm going to make a machine that will make bigger beads!" Dub declared.

He recognized the problem was that the beads were just too small for little Avy. And so he solved this whole dilemma by coming up with an invention.

"If the beads are bigger," he said, "then Avy can play with them and she won't get in trouble."

I don't know that Avy ever complained about the "Bead Banishment" after that. She looked across the table that night at her hero. A big brother named

Dub that invented something just for her. She never doubted that he would do it. Dub declared that he would build her a machine to make bigger beads, and for Avy it was a done deal.

As a little boy, Dub understands something that most grown men have still yet to figure out. His best energies and strength are best utilized when directed to the rescue and assistance of those around him. He is wired to think like a real man should.

No one at the dinner table that night ever asked me whether bigger beads would cause me to remove my fatherly banishment of beads for little Avonlea Rose. It just seemed obvious to everyone at the table that Dub's thinking was sound and cogent. And I figured if Dub really did invent such a machine, then I wouldn't want to stand in the way of Avy crying out, "Dub, you are my hero!"

INVENTION FOUR

Army Green Nail Polish

There was a movement over a decade ago that sponsored the idea of metro-males. A "metro" was a man who kind of looked and acted like a girl. Let it be known that yours truly was not a fan of this movement. For me, the concept of masculinity and femininity are pretty clear. Men should be men and women should be women.

I teach my kids this way, too. I may not be deemed politically and socially sensitized on this point, but I do take my fatherly duties seriously. I don't want my son forsaking his manliness because his father was trying to build a high popularity rating with society during the years of his development.

As a result, my boys are trained to be gentlemen and my girls are trained to be ladies. And, by the way, that's important in regards to Dub's fourth invention. Because the next day following Dub's amazing Bead-Making Machine, he launched into territory a bit more sketchy.

While I was away at work that day, Dub was at home discovering something new. His five-year-old curiosity was piqued. He had overheard a discussion between Harper and Avy about getting their nails painted on their latest outing with Momma. Dub, fascinated by this concept, explored the idea further and discovered that the girls actually had a bottle of this nail painting stuff in the bathroom.

Dub's mind was swimming with excitement.

He waited for Harper and Avy to venture into another room and then he went to work.

He carefully and quietly removed the lid from the nail polish and found a queer and fascinating little brush inside. He artistically dabbed the brush against his little boy fingernails, then clandestinely screwed the lid back on.

NOTE: There is still the outside possibility that he was not alone in this "painting project," but no other witnesses have come forward to testify of their involvement as of yet.

I arrived home from work, waltzed into the kitchen to the loud greeting of my kids and Gracie the dog, and made my way to the kitchen counter for my nightly ritual of putting away my phone and keys and sifting through the mail.

It was at this precise time that the lid was blown off of Dub's escapades from earlier that afternoon.

"Dub?" said Momma with concern. "Did you put pink nail polish on your fingernails?"

Dub hid his fingers from view and mumbled something inaudible. His gaze danced about the room, from Momma, to Daddy, and then towards the floor, with the clear sign of guilt scribbled upon his features.

Daddy's sifting through the mail stopped abruptly at this.

I strode across the kitchen and towered over the little guy who stood staring awkwardly at the wood floor.

"Let me see those fingers, Buddy!" I said with a paternal firmness.

I moved in to investigate, gently prying those little fingers from beneath the hidden folds of his t-shirt. Sure enough, the little guy had pink nail polish on.

There are moments when we parents should be deeply concerned about the welfare of our children and moments when we really shouldn't. Usually we parents get these two sorts of moments mixed up and get concerned when we should be laughing and we shrug our shoulders nonchalantly when we should be kicking into action.

It's very possible that this was one of those moments when I should have laughed, but there is something in my wiring that, instead, caused me to consider it a moment of dire fragility – a moment that, if not addressed in all the seriousness of fatherly gravity, would result in my little boy would grow up wearing pink nail polish forever and always.

So, Daddy set down the law.

"Dub, boys do NOT wear nail polish!"

Don't get me wrong; I wasn't harsh towards the little dude. I was just really straight-forward. I was "to the point." It was my way of saying, "You, my boy, are not going to be one of those metros!"

But Dub didn't quite interpret my concern the way I intended it. He knew Daddy was not a fan of the color pink blended with manhood. So, in his inventive little mind, he began to concoct an idea – a way of solving this dilemma.

After all, to him the problem wasn't the nail polish; it was the color pink in the nail polish.

So, as the thought began to awaken within his Edison-like mind, he began to turn his gaze from the floor to my face. No longer was there shame, but confidence. The little guy transformed from sheepish to strong in a matter of seconds.

"Daddy!" he stated with bold assurance. "I've got an idea!"

In his manner, I even got the notion that he was giving me a morsel of marvel that he fully expected to change my life as a father, as a husband, and as a man.

Without even a pause, he let the idea fly. It filled the entire kitchen with the magnanimity that Dub uniquely possesses.

"I'm going to make a nail polish for boys," he declared; "one that is a boy color, so that boys can wear it too."

You could hear it in his voice. He was saying, in his own precious way, "Daddy, you could wear it too, then!" The sincerity was striking; the genuine affectation for men to share in this amazing privilege of nail-polish-wearing was a sight to behold. He'd personally tasted the beauty of it and now he had a way of sharing it with all of us boys who were utterly deprived due to the pinkish coloring of the stuff.

Now I know that all of you are wanting to know how I responded to this. After all, if this really is one of those moments of dire fragility, then army green nail polish isn't going to solve that problem. Let it be said that Dub's inventions are very therapeutic for helping correct my propensity toward paternal over-reaction. These crazy ideas have a way of bringing me back down into the realm of little kid reality and helping me to laugh when I might otherwise consider banning Dub from conversing with Harper and Avy ever again, lest he start inventing army green lipstick next.

I can't say that I laughed out loud at the nail polish invention, but I did laugh. And I immediately went and wrote it down, recording it as the fourth official Dandy Dub Invention. That says something, isn't it?

Army Green Nail Polish? I honestly hope it never succeeds. However, what Dub's Army Green Nail Polish shows me as a father is to never override innocence in an attempt to save my children from perversion. There is something about innocent invention that must never be quashed. For Dub sees things with a pure perspective, and his inventions, though odd, show a desire to build a world that doesn't hinder anyone from receiving the "good news." And that is something I don't want to ever harm.

His version of "good news" needs to be a bit refined. His gospel of "Hey, men! You too can wear nail polish!" isn't quite the message I'm wanting him to land on. But the idea of sharing the good stuff with everyone, when properly harnessed, I'm certain, will one day lead to, "Hey, world! You too can wear Jesus Christ!"

Now, I really like that!

INVENTION FIVE

Weal Meat Costumes

It was ten days before Christmas in 2013 when Dub whipped out his fifth invention.

But this particular one was captured and recorded for all posterity by his teacher, Miss Cristina. Dub calls her Mit Cwithtina. And Mit Cwithtina is a fellow lover of Dub ingenuity, so when this invention went airborne, she was careful to preserve its profundity for time immemorial.

As the story goes, Dub and Cwithtina were having a little chat. Dub was sharing with his beloved teacher the latest developments of the theme park that he was going to be building soon.

Its name? Dub Ludy Films Land, of course. After all, Walt Disney named a park after himself, why can't Dub do the same?

But the discussion was about a particular exhibit that Dub was planning to build in the park. I'll let Miss Cristina take it from here. This is what she wrote to us in her weekly report about Dub the

Friday of that particular week:

> *Dub told me about an exhibit that he's going to make at "Dubs Ludy Film Land" that involves all the dangerous animals. There's going to be glass all around it that you won't be able to see and spaces where you can go between the clear, glass walls so that it seems like you're right up close to the animals. And you'll have to wear a costume that's made out of meat (not just looks like meat but that "for weal" is meat so that the animals will come to you and then you can take pieces off of your costume and feed them). He also informed me that he and Daddy will be the ones catching all of these dangerous animals. They'll sneak up on them, put a net over them, push them into a cage, and then carry them back to Dubs Ludy Film Land since they're both very strong.*

I've always cherished this as my personal favorite of Dub's Dandy Inventions. It's possible that I'm biased towards it because it's an invention that he dreamed up that involves Daddy and Dub working side-by-side together to catch, cloister, and feed dangerous animals. But I also like it because it's strangely profound.

I'm a guy who deals with the message of the Gospel day-in-day-out. So, when I hear Dub's invention, I see something in it that is truly remarkable. And it gives me, as a father, an insight into Dub's purpose here on earth.

The Gospel of Jesus Christ is strangely, and even remarkably, a "weal meat" costume. You must be in this "weal meat" and you must have this "weal meat" in you. Even Jesus, in John chapter six says,

"For my flesh is 'weal' food and my blood is 'weal' drink." NOTE: of course, it's supposed to be the word "real" and not "weal," but I'm making a point here. And then, after this shocking statement, Jesus adds, "He that eats My flesh, and drinks My blood, dwells in Me, and I in him."

I don't know that Dub's idea of he and I wearing "weal meat costumes" is any more or less odd than Jesus' statements back 2,000 years ago to the people of Israel. We, as Christians, have been given something very real and life-changing. Like the wild animals at Dub Ludy Films Land, we've been given "weal meat" – we've been given the life of Jesus Christ to change our wildness into wisdom, our self-centeredness into selflessness.

Dub's vision, at this juncture of his life, is to take the Gospel of Jesus Christ to North Korea when he grows up. I don't know that he really understands how impossible such a mission is, but I hold his yearning as precious. And it is also not lost on me that what is impossible with man is possible with God. So, maybe the Dooster and I will someday venture together into the untamed lands of North Korea to hand to the hungry souls of that wild territory the Bread of Heaven.

INVENTION FIVE, SIX, SEVEN, EIGHT, NINE, AND TEN

Five Year Olds Think of the Darnedest Things

Over the next two weeks, Dub went on an invention spree, knocking out the sixth, seventh, eighth, ninth, and tenth inventions in his dandy collection.

Dub's sixth invention was the Robot Refrigerator Machine. This was designed at Nana and Pop's place. This multi-purpose contraption is an all-in-one refrigerator savior. First, it puts away all your groceries. And as Dub would say, "Its puts the apples with apples and the bananas with bananas." But it does even more than that. Dub, being convinced that "all fridges are dirty," made this handy machine also capable of deep cleaning any and all refrigerators no matter their degree of grime. Wow! Did I hear someone say, "Kickstarter"? Dub's seventh invention was The Wild West Backyard Amusement Park. I guess Dub has plans to transform the Ludy backyard into a real-life amusement park. Everyone who arrives gets a cowboy costume, a gun, a horse, and a wild-western adventure. It should be interesting to see how our neighborhood association will view this idea. They shot down my backyard shed, so it makes perfect sense that they would be big fans of thousands of random visitors, roller coasters, loud and obnoxious carnival music, and horsey doo-doo all over the place.

Dub's eighth invention was the Doggie Changing Machine. This contraption offers anyone, with the guts and desire to change things up a bit in life, to become a dog. And, it's fairly simple to operate. If you enter the machine, you become a dog – and any kind of dog you would like. Big dogs, little dogs, yippy dogs – it doesn't matter. Dub's got the device to make it all happen. And for those wondering how they might get back to human state if the season as a doggy didn't go as well as hoped, then all that is necessary is entering back inside the Doggy Changing Machine.

Dub's ninth invention was The Hair Machine. This device grows hair anywhere you might need it. You feeling a little insecure about your hairless elbow? From what I understand, Dubber's Dandy Hair Machine can solve your problem in a jiffy and supply you with the hairiest elbows on the block.

Dub's tenth invention was The Flying Pack. This

is Dub's super-duper flying machine, guaranteed to give you the thrill of flight. Just hold out your arms, strap this baby to them, slip the jet pack over your neck, and zip-zip-away.

As a father, I love these ideas. Each of them is treasured in my heart. The sheer ridiculousness of some of them, mixed with the outright boyishness of others, makes my father's heart smile. There is something so utterly precious about little kiddo ideas. They aren't barnacled with the mature sensibilities that, those of us of the graying hair persuasion, often carry around. They are innocent, always plausible, and wholly conceivable to the five-year-old mind.

And I'm convinced that this is precisely why Jesus said, "Unless you are converted and become as little children, you will by no means enter the kingdom of heaven."

Jesus might as well have said, "Hey, guys, unless you start thinking like little Dubber-Dooster, you really aren't fit for My Kingdom."

In the Kingdom of Heaven, it is common knowledge that God is able to do anything and everything. There is nothing that is impossible for Him. In fact, those of us that are citizens of this glorious Kingdom can do all things through Christ who gives us strength.

It's amazing, but Dub knows these "kingdom" facts without any bonus Bible college schooling. It's all of us old fogeys that need to once again become like the little Doosty-Dandy and behold afresh that anything is possible for them that believe.

INVENTION ELEVEN

The Fly Into Any Movie Machine

Dub had quite a run of inventions when he was five. It was thirty-eight days of little Einstein around the Ludy home, and out popped eleven dandy inventions. And the final one is arguably the most endearing. Invention number eleven has Dub's personality written all over it. And, outside of my fatherly bias toward the superiority of invention five, this one, I must admit, if it were human, would have the most likes on Facebook.

We were all snuggled warmly on the couch in the Ludy "cozy" room watching an episode of *The Little House on the Prairie* when number eleven crescendoed forth. This particular L.H.O.T.P. episode proved quite stirring to Dub's little soul. It was about a little girl name Olga who walked with a limp. She always sat on the fringe and was generally left out of everything. Since she couldn't run and play, she would sit and watch the other kids run and play. Olga needed a friend.

Dub couldn't stand it anymore. About ten minutes into the episode, Dub was bursting with concern. So, without further ado, and without waiting to see what might transpire in the episode, Dub went to work. And out popped invention number eleven.

It's called The Fly Into Any Movie Machine. It reminds me a lot of Bert's sidewalk chalk drawings in Mary Poppins. I don't know how he did it, but Dub found a porthole – he discovered the way into the movies. And with Dub's dandy invention, you, me, and even Gracie the dog can hop into a movie and rescue someone in need.

Olga needed a rescuer, and Dub figured out a way that he could help her.

It's interesting because Dub knows he's adopted. And it almost seems that with that knowledge comes a desire to serve anyone and everyone who finds themselves in need of a family. He's a little guy who can't sit by idly while Olga is suffering. He must do something.

What if we all were this way? What if each one of us went to work inventing solutions the moment we saw someone in need and did whatever we could do to help them?

Dub may not realize how profound his vision to help Olga really is. With 163 million orphans in need of someone to "fly" into their life to help them, I think Dub's on to something.

We, the Church of Jesus Christ, need something – a tool with which to help these precious limping children. We need a machine, a device, a contraption, a thingamajig – we need an invention. And though this might seem a bit strange, I would like to submit the idea that I believe God already has invented this much-needed device. It's called adoption.

Adoption may not necessarily be novel and new, but it sure is tried, trusty, and true. And, better yet, it's a God invention. Which means it's guaranteed to work, redeem, and alter the course of history. And, from personal experience, I can say that it changes the lives of those who simply say "yes" to its heavenly brilliance.

I'm writing this book nearly fourteen months after Dub put the finishing touches to his eleventh invention. He's now working on invention #163.* The little guy seems to be aiming for his 1,500th by the time he graduates high-school. Go, Dub!

So, while Dub is busy working on invention #163, I'd like the rest of us to do some serious thinking and start working on God's #163 – 163,000,000 orphans, that is.

Would you please consider doing something about this issue? It doesn't even have to be something big – but please consider doing something.

There are countless little Dubs out there in this great big wide world who are simply needing a momma and a daddy to step forward and start loving them. Sure, all these little Dubs come

---

* This is a rough estimate based on the factor of eleven inventions every 5 weeks, with a slight inflationary statistic figured in to compensate for his ever-maturing inventive capacity. The guy is an invention machine.

prepackaged with their eccentricities, their funny quirks, their mischievous grins, and their rascally tendencies – but they also come as living lessons of the heartbeat of Father God.

I am privileged to be able to call Dub my son. I realize his name may not be the most obvious choice for the U.S. presidency, but maybe that is because his calling far exceeds that of mere politics. I believe that "Dub" is an ideal name for a man ready to give himself wholly and fully to the call of the Gospel – to live, and even die, giving hope to the dying, befriending the friendless, sharing Truth with those shrouded in lies.

Can't you just see it? In twenty-five years from now, the headline reads:

Dub Ludy, a Man for Such a Time as This

Such are the dreams of an adoptive father whose buttons are bursting with love.

Please consider loving a "Dub" all your own. There is simply nothing quite like it.

The fun thing about little dudes like Dub is that they are nuclear blessings. You may think at first that you are reaching out to help them, when, in fact, as the story unfolds, it will be shown that likely the real reason God put these precious miracles in our lives was to rescue us.

Made in the USA
Middletown, DE
23 April 2024